Grades 2–3

ACTIVITIES FOR
FAST FINISHERS
LANGUAGE ARTS

**55 Reproducible Puzzles, Brain Teasers, and Other
Independent, Learning-Rich Activities Kids Can't Resist!**

by Jan Meyer

New York • Toronto • London • Auckland • Sydney **Teaching**
Mexico City • New Delhi • Hong Kong • Buenos Aires *Resources*

FOR JEFFREY, JULIA, JAMIE, AND SIERRA

Editor: Mela Ottaiano
Cover design: Brian LaRossa
Interior design: Melinda Belter
Interior illustrations: Teresa Anderko

ISBN-13: 978-0-545-15985-2
ISBN-10: 0-545-15985-7

Copyright © 2010 by Jan Meyer
All rights reserved. Published by Scholastic Inc.
Printed in the U.S.A.

1 2 3 4 5 6 7 8 9 10   40   17 16 15 14 13 12 11 10

TABLE OF CONTENTS

FUN WITH WORDS

ANSWERS

ABOUT THIS BOOK

Teachers frequently ask, "What, other than silent reading, can I use to keep fast finishers productively busy?" This book has been designed to address this concern.

- There are 55 pages of engaging language arts activities.
- Fast finishers can work on these activities independently.
- A relatively short period of time is required to complete most of these activities.

The activities in this book cover topics you teach in your classroom: spelling, vocabulary, and a wide variety of language skills. They provide practice with synonyms, antonyms, contractions, compound words, syllables, prefixes, suffixes, alphabetical order, capitalization, and more. There's also a large section of wordplay activities that stimulate an enjoyment of words—their formation, spelling patterns, and sounds. Not your ordinary fill-in-the-blanks exercises, these child-pleasing activities include scrambled words, words within words, crossword puzzles, riddles to solve, secret letter codes, and a broad array of other types of puzzles.

Students of varying abilities can enjoy these activities. For those who need some help with certain skill areas, some pages have examples, letter clues, an answer box, or a special "handy hints" section. For students with high-level skills, a number of pages include a "Bonus!" activity for an added challenge.

Name _____

Date _____

Jellyfish Beach

Norton Noun and Vera Verb are spending a sunny day at Jellyfish Beach. Look at the words in the word box. Then write the eight words that are nouns on Norton's beach blanket. Write the eight words that are action verbs on Vera's beach blanket.

follow	friend	hat	bring
leave	vegetable	read	lake
eat	glasses	circus	ask
glove	speak	lion	write

Name _____

Date _____

Yesterday's Crossword

Turn today into yesterday in this crossword puzzle of verbs! Each puzzle clue gives an action that is happening now (a present-tense verb). Each puzzle answer is the same action as it happened yesterday (a past-tense verb).

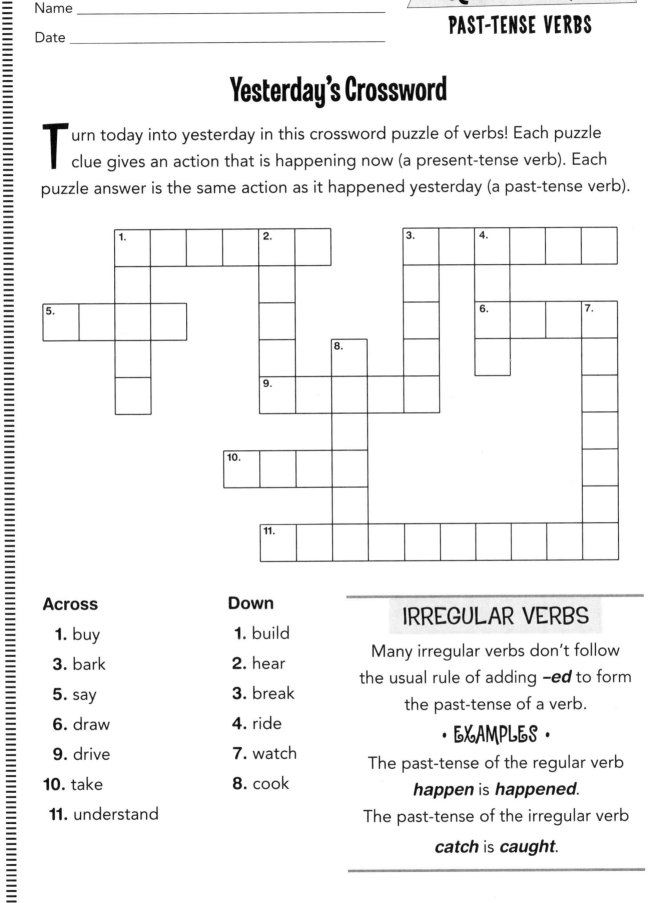

Across

1. buy
3. bark
5. say
6. draw
9. drive
10. take
11. understand

Down

1. build
2. hear
3. break
4. ride
7. watch
8. cook

IRREGULAR VERBS

Many irregular verbs don't follow the usual rule of adding **–ed** to form the past-tense of a verb.

• EXAMPLES •

The past-tense of the regular verb **happen** is **happened**.

The past-tense of the irregular verb **catch** is **caught**.

You've Got Mail

All of the capital letters are missing from these vacation postcards. Can you find all of the words that need capitals? Draw a circle around each word that should begin with a capital letter.

dear aunt lisa and uncle jeff,

we're having a wonderful time here in florida. yesterday we went to disneyland and spent the whole day there. the weather is so beautiful and warm that it's hard to believe that it's march.

love,

jason

mr. and mrs. moore
127 maple drive
newton, maine 11865

hi tony,

new york is a very exciting city. on friday we went to the museum of natural history. the dinosaur displays are what keesha and i liked best. yesterday we watched the parade that they have here each thanksgiving. there were huge balloons and even a santa claus.

denzel

tony milano
3380 baker street
rockland, ohio 22714

Name _____

Date _____

Rhyme Finds

Draw a line under each of the ten words at the right that rhyme with *smear*. Now find and circle the ten rhyming words you underlined. The words go across (→) and down (↓).

hear	cheer	bear	dear	rear
here	their	clear	near	pear
there	year	wear	deer	fear

r	e	a	r	b	l	e	m	f	a	e	r
c	a	m	i	l	d	s	o	o	w	b	e
y	l	u	f	e	e	r	c	h	e	e	r
s	o	v	e	t	a	d	e	a	l	a	e
n	p	w	a	i	r	h	x	e	e	r	d
g	h	e	r	o	p	e	a	r	s	i	e
m	a	y	o	u	e	r	s	t	e	d	e
o	n	e	l	r	k	e	y	o	w	a	p
t	e	a	m	e	e	r	c	l	e	a	r
e	a	r	j	d	e	e	r	e	a	c	h
z	r	u	e	o	r	g	m	w	r	o	e
c	a	t	h	e	a	r	l	o	v	a	q

RHYMING WORDS

* Not all words that rhyme have the same spelling pattern.

EXAMPLE: I *heard* a *bird* say a *word*.

* Not all words with the same spelling pattern rhyme.

EXAMPLE: He *said* he had *paid*.

Name _____

Date _____

Rhyme Scrambles

Unscramble each word and write it on the line to the right. Some of these scrambled words can make several different words, but you must make a word that rhymes with all of the words in the group.

1. t h i e g   _eight_

    t e a   _____

    i t w a   _____

2. l l r o   _____

    h l e o   _____

    w b o l   _____

3. r f o   _____

    m r o e   _____

    o o d r   _____

    u o f r   _____

4. y r c   _____

    e e y   _____

    e i p   _____

    h h g i   _____

5. w o t   _____

    u e b l   _____

    h s e o   _____

    w e r g   _____

6. h i r a   _____

    e a r p   _____

    c r e a   _____

    h e r e w   _____

RHYMING WORDS

* Not all words that rhyme have the same spelling pattern.

• EXAMPLE •

The word **cheer** rhymes with **here** and **gear** and **pier**.

* Not all words with the same spelling pattern rhyme.

• EXAMPLE •

The word **bear** does not rhyme with **near**.

Activities for Fast Finishers: Language Arts © 2010 by Jan Meyer, Scholastic Teaching Resources

SIMILES

Name _____

Date _____

As Tasty as . . . Worm Soup?

The simile in the title of this page seems completely wrong. Wouldn't as tasty as a slice of cake be better? Draw a line to the word that fits best in each of these similes.

1. as gentle as a   elf

2. as hard as a   mountain

3. as sweet as   ice

4. as loud as a   clown

5. as light as a   lamb

6. as bright as the   rock

7. as high as a   sun

8. as funny as a   honey

9. as tiny as an   balloon

10. as cold as   drum

SIMILE

A phrase or figure of speech that compares two things using the words **as** or **like** is called a **simile**.

• EXAMPLE •

as rough as sandpaper

Bonus!   Create your own similes by completing each of the phrases below.

a. as big as a/an _____

b. as quick as a/an _____

c. as soft as a/an _____

d. as tasty as a/an _____

Name _____

Date _____

Something in Common

Ladybugs, bees, and mosquitoes have things in common. They all can fly, they all have six legs, and they are all insects. Spiders are different and don't belong with this group. Spiders have eight legs, they can't fly, and they aren't insects. Circle the three words in each row that you think have something in common. Then write on the line what these three words have in common.

EXAMPLE: (crayon)   paper   (pencil)   (pen)

They are all things to write with.

1.   boots   scarf   mittens   shorts

_____

2.   dog   kitten   lamb   piglet

_____

3.   sofa   chair   table   stool

_____

4.   leaves   roots   stems   dirt

_____

5.   barn   subway   cow   scarecrow

_____

6.   Texas   Alaska   Chicago   Florida

_____

Name _____

Date _____

Finding Relationships

Complete each analogy using a word from the word box.

scales	painting	milk	sit	wood
winter	princess	smell	hand	goal

1. bed is to lie as chair is to _____

2. ear is to hear as nose is to _____

3. shoe is to foot as mitten is to _____

4. hammer is to nail as saw is to _____

5. bird is to feathers as fish is to _____

6. hen is to eggs as cow is to _____

7. king is to queen as prince is to _____

8. author is to book as artist is to _____

9. baseball is to a run as soccer is to a _____

10. bathing suit is to summer as snowsuit is to _____

Bonus!   See if you can finish these analogies.

a. oink is to pig as _____

b. apple is to fruit as _____

ANALOGY

An *analogy* is a special way to show the relationship between two sets of words. In an analogy, the second pair of words must have the same relationship as the words in the first pair of words.

• EXAMPLE •
kitten is to *cat* as *puppy* is to *dog*
(A kitten is a baby cat and a puppy is a baby dog.)

Tap 'Em, Snap 'Em, Clap 'Em!

Here's a great way to find out how many syllables a word has. Just say the word while you tap your foot, snap your fingers, or clap your hands with each beat of the word. Try it!

bat (tap)   **hap•py (snap•snap)**   **ba•na•na (clap•clap•clap)**

Clap, tap, or snap each word in the box below. Write one-syllable words in the square, two-syllable words in the circle, three-syllable words in the rectangle.

alphabet	stuff	ghost	magician	table
earth	winter	airplane	prize	crocodile
chimpanzee	dime	balloon	calendar	chicken

1-Syllable Words

2-Syllable Words

Bonus!

On the back of the page, draw a shape and write your own four-syllable words in it!

3-Syllable Words

Name _____

Date _____

The Syllable Shuffler

Snarg the syllable shuffler has mixed up the two syllables of these words. In each group below, draw a line from a syllable in the left column to a syllable in the column next to it to form a word. Write the five words you've formed on the lines in the box.

cor •   • nic

car •   • kin

nap •   • rect

mir •   • rot

pic •   • ror

correct
_____
_____
_____
_____

pa •   • low

blan •   • ther

mon •   • per

pil •   • ket

bro •   • ster

_____
_____
_____
_____
_____

jun •   • dle

un •   • ble

ta •   • tle

cra •   • gle

cat •   • cle

_____
_____
_____
_____
_____

Name _____

Date _____

Contraction Action

A contraction is a fast way to join two words together. One or more letters in the second word are left out and replaced by an apostrophe.

EXAMPLE: *there is* becomes *there's*

Write in the missing words or contractions.

1. _____was_____ + not = wasn't

2. I + am = _____

3. is + _____ = isn't

4. here + is = _____

5. you + _____ = you're

6. _____ + not = doesn't

7. they + have = _____

8. we + will = _____

9. should + _____ = should've

10. let + us = _____

11. who + is = _____

12. you + would = _____

13. who + _____ = who've

14. we + are = _____

Activities for Fast Finishers: Language Arts © 2010 by Jan Meyer, Scholastic Teaching Resources

Name _____

Date _____

Commas for California

Michelle has written a very good report, but it is missing all of the needed commas. That's because the comma key on her computer keyboard is broken. Can you find all of the places where commas are needed? Add the missing commas to this report.

California

by Michelle Andrews

My grandparents live in Sacramento California. That is the capital of the state of California. The largest city in this state is Los Angeles. The state has more than 35000000 people.

California ranks as the third biggest state in area and the largest state in population. It became our country's 31st state on September 9 1850. California is called the Golden State. A grizzly bear is on its state flag.

California has beaches mountains forests and a large desert area. Many different crops are grown in this state. They include strawberries lemons walnuts apricots and grapes.

Our first stop this summer vacation will be Reno Nevada. Then we are driving to Sacramento to visit my grandparents. We are also going to go to San Francisco. This California city has steep hills cable cars beautiful parks and a place called Fisherman's Wharf. A special sight in this city is the Golden Gate Bridge. It opened on May 27 1937. I can't wait to see it.

COMMAS

USE COMMAS TO . . .	EXAMPLE
separate the date in a month from the year	July 3, 1827
separate the name of a city and a state	Dallas, Texas
separate words in a series of three or more	chairs, tables, beds, and sofas
separate digits in a number in order to show hundreds, thousands, millions, etc.	4,300,000

Name _____

Date _____

Three in a Row

In each puzzle there are three words in a row that all have a short vowel sound or a long vowel sound. Find the correct row and draw a line through the words in it. The row can go across (→), down (↓), or diagonally (↘).

1. Find three words in a row with a short vowel sound.

chat	cow	film
skunk	swing	tail
for	dust	dress

2. Find three words in a row with a long vowel sound.

place	goose	boy
crush	point	chief
smile	mean	hay

3. Find three words in a row with a long vowel sound.

steam	quick	meat
bark	glow	cute
quite	state	mouse

4. Find three words in a row with a short vowel sound.

stay	lunch	strength
wish	track	what
soup	bread	apple

5. Find three words in a row with a short vowel sound.

egg	print	hurt
quit	third	lost
dance	change	laugh

6. Find three words in a row with a long vowel sound.

right	cheese	ghost
through	school	worse
eight	sense	child

CONSONANT BLENDS

Name _____

Date _____

One for All

Fill in the blanks, but just one of the consonant blends will do. That's because only one of the choices can make a word with each of the three word parts. In each row, fill in the blanks with the **one** consonant blend that makes sense with all three word parts.

1. __sk__ ip   __sk__ ill   __sk__ ate

ch	pl	sk

2. ____ ade   ____ ust   ____ ee

sh	bl	tr

3. ____ ing   ____ eep   ____ im

sw	br	st

4. ____ ock   ____ own   ____ ap

tr	bl	cl

5. ____ ush   ____ ain   ____ ick

cr	tr	br

6. ____ eam   ____ op   ____ ore

ch	pl	st

7. ____ ow   ____ ide   ____ ip

gl	sl	fl

8. ____ ot   ____ eed   ____ ell

bl	tw	sp

Name _____

Date _____

Fantastic Finishes

Let your imagination run wild as you write a fantastic finish for each of these sentence starters.

1. The wizard _____

_____

2. I laughed and laughed when _____

_____

3. Last night I dreamed that _____

_____

4. If I had wings and could fly, I would _____

_____

5. I wish _____

_____

Bonus!   Pick one of your sentences and illustrate it below.

Activities for Fast Finishers: Language Arts © 2010 by Jan Meyer, Scholastic Teaching Resources

Scrambled Sentences

Aprankster scrambled the words in each of the sentences on this page. Now the sentences don't make sense. Write each sentence with the words in their correct order on the line below it. Be sure to start each sentence with a capital letter and end it with a period.

EXAMPLE: cat the chased dog the

The dog chased the cat.

1. girls game their won baseball the

_____

2. sweater she new her wore

_____

3. horse cowboy his rode on the

_____

4. the barked man the dog at

_____

5. wonderful apple smells pie that

_____

6. the was hot it beach at

_____

7. park we're the to amusement going

_____

8. arm ant her crawled an up

_____

That's Funny!

Put the words in alphabetical order.
Then find the answer to a silly riddle.

1. ____ ____ ____ ____ ____
                    4

2. ____ ____ ____ ____ ____
         10

3. ____ ____ ____ ____
                         7

4. ____ ____ ____ ____
         2

5. ____ ____ ____ ____ ____
    9

6. ____ ____ ____ ____ ____
              8

7. ____ ____ ____ ____ ____
         5

8. ____ ____ ____ ____ ____
              3

9. ____ ____ ____ ____ ____
                         1

10. ____ ____ ____ ____ ____
                    6

dance	fruit
brush	dusty
chart	every
beach	drink
first	above

ABC ORDER

If the first letter of two
or more words is the
same, compare the
second letters.

• **EXAMPLE** •

bag comes before **big**

Write the numbered letters on the correct lines
to solve the riddle.

On what side does a duck have the most feathers?

____ ____ ____ ____ ____ ____ ____ ____ ____ ____
 1   2   3   4   5   6   7   8   9   10

Activities for Fast Finishers: Language Arts © 2010 by Jan Meyer, Scholastic Teaching Resources

That's Funny, Too!

Put the words in alphabetical order.
Then find the answer to a silly riddle.

1. ___ ___ ___ ___ ___
                    7

2. ___ ___ ___ ___ ___
                        10

3. ___ ___ ___ ___ ___
              4

4. ___ ___ ___ ___ ___
                8

5. ___ ___ ___ ___ ___
        1

6. ___ ___ ___ ___ ___
        6

7. ___ ___ ___ ___ ___
                5

8. ___ ___ ___ ___ ___
            2

9. ___ ___ ___ ___ ___
        3

10. ___ ___ ___ ___ ___
              9

names	panda
owner	patch
match	money
magic	paste
mouth	place

ABC ORDER

* If the first letter of
two or more words is
the same, compare the
second letters.
* If the second letters are
also the same, compare
the third letters.

• EXAMPLES •

ball comes before bell
find comes before fist

Write the numbered letters from the word list on the correct lines to
solve the riddle.

What is a witch at the beach called?

___ ___ ___ ___ ___ ___ ___ ___ ___ ___
 1   2   3   4   5   6   7   8   9   10

Activities for Fast Finishers: Language Arts © 2010 by Jan Meyer, Scholastic Teaching Resources

Name _____

Date _____

What's In-Between?

Here are two pages from a dictionary of animal life. Using the guide words, circle the words that will be on each of these pages.

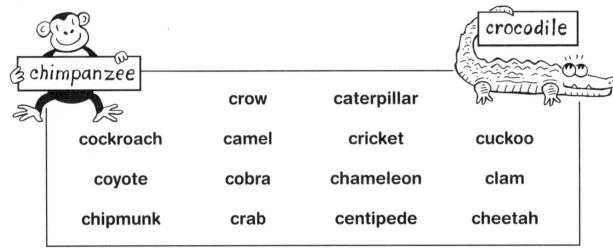

chimpanzee   **crocodile**

	crow	caterpillar	
cockroach	camel	cricket	cuckoo
coyote	cobra	chameleon	clam
chipmunk	crab	centipede	cheetah

seal   **squirrel**

	salamander	skunk	
	snail	sponge	
	swordfish	snake	
shark	scorpion	shrimp	stork
squid	starfish	spider	sheep

GUIDE WORDS

At the top of every dictionary page, the guide word on the left is the first word defined on the page. The word on the right is the last. The words on the dictionary page come in ABC order between the guide words.

• EXAMPLE •

If the guide words are **down** and **dust**, the word **duck** will be on the page. The word **dog** will not be on the page.

Activities for Fast Finishers: Language Arts © 2010 by Jan Meyer, Scholastic Teaching Resources

Name _____

Date _____

Buzzy, the Spelling Bee

Buzzy, the spelling bee, has flown into a field in which all of the flowers have misspelled words in their centers. Write the correct spelling for each word on the line under each flower.

pleeze   evry   agin

_____ _____ _____

famly   shoud   anser

_____ _____ _____

offen   becuz   eazy

_____ _____ _____

Name _____

Date _____

Can You Spell Well?

Circle each word in the word box that is misspelled. Then write the correct spelling for each of these words on the lines below.

surprise	people	freind	Teusday	whoze
Saturday	enough	minit	allways	beautiful
nieghbor	vegetable	doller	before	February
berthday	listen	amung	adress	Wednesday
piece	recieve	sommer	quick	any

_____   _____   _____

_____   _____   _____

_____   _____   _____

_____   _____   _____

SPELLING RULES FOR "I" AND "E"

The letter **i** comes before **e** except after the letter **c** or when it sounds like **a** as in *weigh*.

• EXAMPLES •
tie, **receive**, and **neigh**

Activities for Fast Finishers: Language Arts © 2010 by Jan Meyer, Scholastic Teaching Resources

Name _____

Date _____

They're Hoping to Go Shopping

You can add the endings *–ing* or *–ed* to most words by simply placing them at the end of the words. But that's not true when you add *–ing* or *–ed* to *hope* or to *shop.* Write the missing words in the table below.

	Base Word	-ing	-ed
1.	save		saved
2.	look	looking	
3.		rubbing	rubbed
4.		living	
5.			wished
6.	learn		
7.	stir		
8.			danced
9.		flipping	
10.	bake		

ADDING -ING AND -ED

* If a word ends in a **silent e**, drop the **e** before adding **–ing** or **–ed**.

EXAMPLE: **trade** becomes **trading** or **traded**

* If a word ends in a **single vowel** followed by a **single consonant**, double the final consonant before adding **–ing** or **–ed**.

EXAMPLE: **bat** becomes **batting** or **batted**.

Double Trouble

Ten words have reported that their double consonants are missing! In each row of the chart, fill in the correct missing double consonant. Then write the completed word. Some of the double consonants are used more than once.

bb	dd	ff	gg	ll	rr	ss	tt

Missing Double Consonant	Completed Word
1. l e ____ ____ o n	
2. g i ____ ____ l e	
3. t r a ____ ____ i c	
4. c h e ____ ____ y	
5. b u ____ ____ l e	
6. p a ____ ____ l e	
7. m u ____ ____ i n	
8. r i ____ ____ o n	
9. l i ____ ____ l e	
10. y e ____ ____ o w	

Bonus! Find five or more words that end with the double consonant *–ss*. Write them on the back of this sheet of paper.

Activities for Fast Finishers: Language Arts © 2010 by Jan Meyer, Scholastic Teaching Resources

Name _____

Date _____

Lions, Foxes, Monkeys, and Ponies

Most plural nouns are formed by adding an **s** at the end of the word, but some nouns have special rules. Complete the crossword puzzle by filling in the plural for each of the nouns in the across and down clues.

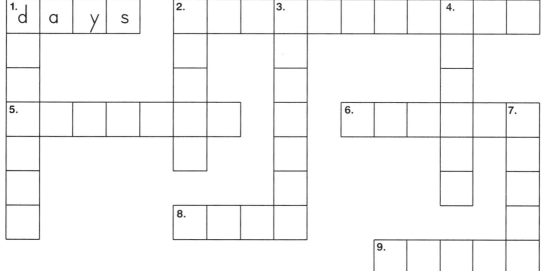

Across

1. day

2. butterfly

5. glass

6. dish

8. toy

9. bus

Down

1. dragon

2. box

3. turkey

4. inch

7. step

PLURAL NOUNS

IF A WORD ENDS IN . . .

ch, **sh**, **x**, **s**, **ss**, or **zz**, add **es** at the end of the word.

a *consonant* followed by a **y**, change the **y** to **i** and add **es**.

a *vowel* followed by a **y**, just add an **s**.

EXAMPLE

The plural of **dress** is **dresses**. The plural of **beach** is **beaches**.

The plural of **puppy** is **puppies**. The plural of **baby** is **babies**.

The plural of **tray** is **trays**. The plural of **boy** is **boys**.

Name _____

Date _____

Help! Help!

A hungry, word-eating shark swam into the synonyms below and ate all but one of the letters in each. Put the letters back in each of these words to make a word that is a synonym of the word to its left.

1. simple   __ __ s __

2. yell   __ h __ __ __

3. begin   __ __ a __ __

4. big   __ __ r __ __

5. choose   __ __ __ k

6. angry   __ a __

7. quick   __ __ __ t

8. gift   __ __ __ __ __ t

9. difficult   __ a __ __

10. frighten   __ c __ __ __

11. ill   __ __ __ k

SYNONYMS

Synonyms are words that have the same or nearly the same meaning as another word.

EXAMPLE: *nearly* and *almost*

Activities for Fast Finishers: Language Arts © 2010 by Jan Meyer, Scholastic Teaching Resources

Ted's Terrible Tuesday

Ted needs your help! Change his terrible Tuesday into a terrific Tuesday by rewriting the story on the lines below. Change each underlined word in the story to its antonym.

Ted's Terrible Tuesday

Ted was feeling <u>sad</u>. Today was Amy's party and he was going to wear <u>old</u> jeans and a <u>dirty</u> t-shirt. On his way to the party Ted <u>lost</u> a five-dollar bill. When he arrived, <u>no one</u> was <u>inside</u> playing games. The games were <u>boring</u>. Ted was the <u>slowest</u> runner in the relay races and his team <u>lost</u>.

<u>Before</u> the games, it was time to eat. Ted was <u>full</u>. He had pizza, a <u>small</u> piece of cake, and some <u>hot</u> lemonade. At the <u>beginning</u> of the party Ted said to Amy, "That was one of the <u>worst</u> parties I've ever gone to. I'm <u>sorry</u> I came."

Ted's Terrific Tuesday

Ted was feeling happy.

_____

_____

_____

_____

_____

_____

ANTONYMS

Antonyms are words that have the opposite meaning of another word.

EXAMPLE: *empty* and *full*

Name _____

Date _____

Huge and Enormous, or Enormous and Tiny

In each row, circle the two words that are synonyms or antonyms.
On the line at the end of the row, write an *S* if the two words are synonyms or an *A* if the two words are antonyms.

#					
1.	always	today	week	never	A
2.	question	book	answer	teacher	
3.	puzzle	part	piece	pie	
4.	place	riddle	middle	center	
5.	thin	tall	body	short	
6.	smart	intelligent	think	book	
7.	night	sleep	sun	day	
8.	swim	water	sink	float	
9.	stop	jump	quit	sign	
10.	bed	asleep	morning	awake	
11.	help	polite	rude	sorry	
12.	laugh	funny	giggle	joke	

Bonus! On the back of this page, draw a picture of the words in one of the pairs of antonyms that you circled.

Activities for Fast Finishers: Language Arts © 2010 by Jan Meyer, Scholastic Teaching Resources

Name _____

Date _____

Which Witch Is Which?

The word pairs below sound the same, but have different spellings and different meanings. Complete each sentence with the correct homophones.

HOMOPHONES

These are words that sound the same as other words, but have different spellings and different meanings.

EXAMPLE: *their* and *there*

1. **tail/tale**   Ali read a _____ about a squirrel who lost his bushy _____.

2. **bored/board**   Jessica was _____ with playing the _____ game.

3. **rode/road**   The boy on the bicycle _____ down the country _____.

4. **through/threw**   Joel won a goldfish when he _____ a ball _____ the loop.

5. **meet/meat**   Let's _____ in the _____ section of the supermarket.

6. **right/write**   Don't forget to _____ the _____ word on the line.

7. **whether/weather**   I don't know _____ the _____ will be rainy today.

8. **guest/guessed**   Rosa _____ that the _____ would sleep in her room.

Bonus!   What do you call a grizzly that's lost its fur? a _____ _____

Name _____

Date _____

Can a Fly Fly?

Fill in the letters for each homograph that fits the pair of definitions.

1. It's something that used to start a fire.

   It means **to go together well** or **to be the same as**. m a t c h

2. It's a unit of measurement for length.

   It's a part of the body. __ __ __ __

3. It's jewelry that's worn on a finger.

   It's the sound a bell makes. __ __ __ __

4. It's something that shines in the night sky.

   It's someone who plays lead parts in movies. __ __ __ __

5. It's a very short measurement of time.

   It's the next place after first place. __ __ __ __ __ __

6. It's something you might hear a dog do.

   It's a covering on a tree. __ __ __ __

7. It's often used to hold lemonade or milk.

   It's a position in baseball. __ __ __ __ __ __

8. It's equal to 36 inches.

   It's the outdoor area in the front or back of houses. __ __ __ __

HOMOGRAPHS

Some words (like *fly*) have the same spelling, but two or more different meanings.

EXAMPLE: When I **miss** breakfast, I stay hungry all day.
I don't **miss** my grouchy Uncle Bert when he travels.

Name _____

Date _____

Cowboy Cal's Compound Roundup

Help Cal round up all of the compound words. Connect words horizontally (→) or vertically (↓). Two have been done for you. Circle the other 12 compound words hidden in the grid below.

cow boy

gold	lake	finger	nail	snake	birth	day	shoe
fish	fast	night	egg	happy	cake	road	lace
dream	rain	every	thing	market	neck	some	jump
funny	snow	smile	place	near	talk	straw	berry
play	ground	where	flash	best	waste	bike	drop
sea	face	mail	light	give	basket	work	sing
shell	map	box	win	hot	boat	fall	class
apple	sauce	toast	base	ball	coat	bird	room

Bonus! Write one sentence with three or more of the words you rounded up.

_____

Compound Connections

Some words start three or more compound words. For example, the word *any* begins the compound words *anyone, anywhere, anybody, anytime, anything, anymore,* and *anyplace.* Write in the word that can be combined with all the words in the row to form three compound words.

1. ___tea___ cup   ___tea___ pot   ___tea___ spoon

2. _____ man   _____ flake   _____ ball

3. _____ coat   _____ bow   _____ drop

4. _____ ache   _____ paste   _____ brush

5. _____ tub   _____ robe   _____ room

6. _____ ball   _____ print   _____ step

7. _____ bell   _____ way   _____ knob

8. _____ tan   _____ shine   _____ burn

9. _____ line   _____ plane   _____ port

10. _____ works   _____ place   _____ truck

Bonus! Pick one of the groups of compounds words you made. Write a sentence using all three words.

_____

_____

Activities for Fast Finishers: Language Arts © 2010 by Jan Meyer, Scholastic Teaching Resources

Looking for Clues

Read each sentence carefully. Then circle the meaning you think is correct for the underlined word based on the context clues for that sentence.

CONTEXT CLUES

When you come across a word you don't know, find out its meaning from the other words around it.

1. Mr. Drone's story was so **tedious** that I almost fell asleep.

   a. exciting   **b.** short   **c.** boring

2. Clare was **astounded** when the magician changed the rabbit into a bird.

   a. angry   **b.** amazed   **c.** tired

3. Mrs. Rosen was **livid** when she discovered that the deer had eaten most of the plants in her garden.

   a. happy   **b.** frightened   **c.** very angry

4. The wonderful **aroma** of the roasting turkey made everyone feel hungry.

   a. size   **b.** sound   **c.** smell

5. A blinding snowstorm made climbing the mountain even more **arduous** for the men.

   a. fun   **b.** difficult   **c.** interesting

6. Jennifer was **elated** when her team won the city soccer championship.

   a. sad   **b.** joyful   **c.** puzzled

Name _____

Date _____

In Other Words

There are many different and more interesting adjectives that can replace the overused ones. On the lines below, write an adjective from the word box or think of your own. Just be sure to follow these rules:

* Don't use **good**, **nice**, **fun**, or **bad**.

* Don't use any adjective more than once.

1. a/an _____ idea

2. a/an _____ party

3. a/an _____ haircut

4. a/an _____ vacation

5. a/an _____ dinner

6. a/an _____ movie

7. a/an _____ smell

8. a/an _____ book

9. a/an _____ game

10. a/an _____ dream

11. a/an _____ neighbor

12. a/an _____ cold

super
horrible
fabulous
extraordinary
pleasant
dull
boring
amazing
exciting
delicious
wonderful
thrilling
great
miserable
enjoyable
tasty
magnificent
marvelous

Activities for Fast Finishers: Language Arts © 2010 by Jan Meyer, Scholastic Teaching Resources

Name _____

Date _____

PREFIXES

That's Amazing!

When the prefix **re-** is put at the beginning of the word **heat**, the word's new meaning is "to heat again." Here are some prefixes that mean "not" or "the opposite of." Write the correct spelling for each new word on the lines below. Then find the amazing answer to a question about crickets.

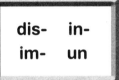

dis-   in-
im-   un

1. not helpful ___ ___ ___ ___ ___ ___ ___ ___ ___ ___
9   11

2. not patient ___ ___ ___ ___ ___ ___ ___ ___ ___
4   2

3. not tied ___ ___ ___ ___ ___ ___
10

4. not correct ___ ___ ___ ___ ___ ___ ___ ___ ___
7   12

5. not honest ___ ___ ___ ___ ___ ___ ___ ___
3   1   14

6. not possible ___ ___ ___ ___ ___ ___ ___ ___ ___ ___
8

7. not agree ___ ___ ___ ___ ___ ___ ___ ___
5   13

8. not fair ___ ___ ___ ___ ___ ___
6

Write the numbered letters from the words on the correct lines to find the answer to this question.

Where are a cricket's ears?

___ ___ ___ ___ ___ ___ ___ ___ ___ ___ ___ ___ ___ ___
1   2   3   4   5   6   7   8   9   10   11 12 13 14

Activities for Fast Finishers: Language Arts © 2010 by Jan Meyer, Scholastic Teaching Resources

39

Even More Amazing!

When the suffix **–ist** is put at the end of the word *art*, the word's new meaning is "someone who does art." Use the suffixes in the box to create new words. Write the correct spelling for each new word on the lines below. Then find the amazing answer to a question about mammals.

SUFFIX	MEANING
-less	**without**
-ous	**full of**
-ful	**full of**

1. full of fear   ___ ___ ___ ___ ___ ___ ___
                          5

2. without power   ___ ___ ___ ___ ___ ___ ___ ___ ___
                        6   3

3. full of poison ___ ___ ___ ___ ___ ___ ___ ___ ___
                                              9

4. full of pain   ___ ___ ___ ___ ___ ___ ___
                              2

5. without care   ___ ___ ___ ___ ___ ___ ___
                          8

6. full of danger ___ ___ ___ ___ ___ ___ ___ ___
                          1

7. full of color   ___ ___ ___ ___ ___ ___ ___
                            4

8. full of thanks ___ ___ ___ ___ ___ ___ ___
                       10 7

Write the numbered letters from the words on the correct lines to find the answer to this question.

What mammal baby spends about two years inside its mother before it's born?

___ ___   ___ ___ ___ ___ ___ ___ ___ ___
 1   2   3   4   5   6   7   8   9   10

Activities for Fast Finishers: Language Arts © 2010 by Jan Meyer, Scholastic Teaching Resources

What's Hiding Inside?

Animal and insect names hide inside words you read all the time. Read the clues in the sentences below. Then use an animal or insect name from the word box to fill in the answer.

hen	ape	moth	eel	owl	cow
crow	cat	bat	rat	bear	lion

1. something that powers some toys   <u>b</u>   <u>a</u>   <u>t</u> t e r y

2. a kind of metal   s t ___ ___ ___

3. a female parent   ___ ___ ___ ___ e r

4. a large number   m i l ___ ___ ___ ___

5. an indoor sport   b ___ ___ ___ i n g

6. Santa has a white one   ___ ___ ___ ___ d

7. someone that is often afraid   ___ ___ ___ a r d

8. a baby toy   ___ ___ ___ t l e

9. a kind of fruit   g r ___ ___ ___

10. a large group of people   ___ ___ ___ ___ d

11. a room in the house   k i t c ___ ___ ___

12. a week at the beach, for example   v a ___ ___ ___ i o n

Mega-Mart Scramble

Take a trip to Mega-Mart, a store where the prices are low but the signs are hard to read. Help make sense of these scrambled words. Unscramble each word below to find five fruits you'll see in the produce section.

s e g r p a   ◯ r ___ p ◯ ___

a a b a n n   ___ ___ ___ ___ ◯ ___

p a l p e   ◯ ___ p ___ ___

e p a r   ___ ___ ___ ◯

e m n o l   m ___ ___ ◯ ___

Now arrange the letters you wrote in the circles to identify one more fruit.

Mega-Mart has a pet section, too. Unscramble each word below to find five pets you'll see there.

t e k i t n   ◯ ___ t ___ ___ ___

s i h f   ___ ___ ◯ ___

n u b y n   ___ ___ ◯ ___ y

a h m s e r t   h ___ ___ ___ ___ ◯ ___

r p a r o t   p ◯ ___ ___ ___ ___

Now arrange the letters you wrote in the circles to find one more pet.

Name _____

Date _____

Shrink 'Ems

Take away one letter from the first word and scramble around the remaining letters to make a four-letter word. Repeat these steps to make a three-letter word and then a two-letter word. In some places, there may be more than one possible answer.

"I'm shrinking!" cried the giant as he became a flying, biting gnat, and then a tiny ant.

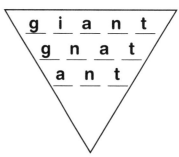

1.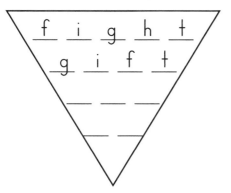

2.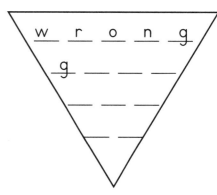

3.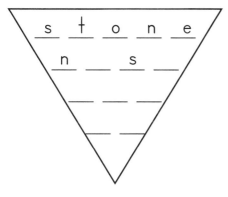

4.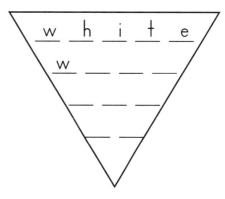

5.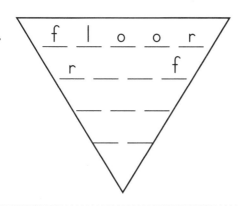

6.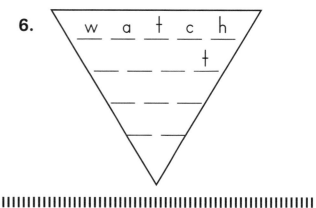

Activities for Fast Finishers: Language Arts © 2010 by Jan Meyer, Scholastic Teaching Resources

The Magic Hat Trick

Put just one word into the magic hat. Twirl your magic wand inside the hat and switch around the letters. Presto Change-O! Out comes a different word. Amazing! Change each underlined word into a new word and write it on the line.

ANAGRAMS

These are words that contain the same letters but are not spelled the same and do not mean the same thing.

• EXAMPLE •

The words **page** and **gape**.

1. Turn **blow** into something you might eat cereal out of. _____

2. Turn **seat** into a direction on a map. _____

3. Turn **grin** into something you might wear on a finger. _____

4. Turn **sale** into an animal that lives in the water. _____

5. Turn **inch** into a part of the face. _____

6. Turn **pea** into a large jungle animal. _____

7. Turn **sore** into a flower. _____

8. Turn **palm** into something that's turned on at night. _____

9. Turn **flow** into an animal that howls. _____

10. Turn **leaf** into a tiny insect. _____

Activities for Fast Finishers: Language Arts © 2010 by Jan Meyer, Scholastic Teaching Resources

Name _____

Date _____

Go Away!

Animals have developed different ways of protecting themselves from their enemies. The skunk sprays. The puffer fish inflates. The hognose snake rolls over and plays dead. To find out what the horned toad does to protect itself, follow the directions for this puzzle. Shade in your answers in the letter grid:

1. the first vowel and the last consonant in the alphabet.

2. all of the consonants in the word **wagon**.

3. all of the vowels in the word **suit**.

4. the consonant that sounds the same as the name of a vegetable that is round and green.

5. the consonant that comes next after the letter **h**.

6. all of the consonants in the word **quart**.

7. the vowel in the word **bed**.

8. the two consonants that are found in **mother**, **home**, and **them**.

9. the consonant that comes next after the letter **t**.

10. all of the consonants in the word **faces**.

11. the silent letter in the word **knot**.

h	v	p	u	w
b	z	l	j	a
r	f	o	c	n
i	k	m	o	d
e	t	g	q	s

Circle the letters that remain. Those letters will spell out the answer to the question below.

Question: What does the horned toad shoot from its eyes when it feels threatened?

Answer: __ __ __ __ __

Name _____

Date _____

Plus One

Pick a letter that will change each of these words into a new word. Write that letter on the line either before or after the plus sign. Then write the new word that you've made on the line after the equal sign.

There's just one rule:

You cannot pick an **s** to put at the end of a word to make it a plural.

1. __b__ + east = ____beast____

2. plan + ____ = _____

3. thin + ____ = _____

4. ____ + care = _____

5. hear + ____ = _____

6. ____ + room = _____

7. crow + ____ = _____

8. star + ____ = _____

9. ____ + read = _____

10. ____ + each = _____

Bonus! Try these super stumpers.

    a. ____ + hole = _____

    b. toot + ____ = _____

Name _____

Date _____

Three Sad Stories

What happened to the letters? Fill in the missing letters to spell a word that fits each clue.

1. Ma and Pa Bumble stumbled into these words and knocked over some of the letters.

the part of the body where food goes	__ __ __ **m a** __ __
the home of a king and queen	**p a** __ __ __ __
something to wear to bed	**p a** __ __ **m a** __
something to write on	**p a** __ __ __
a place where astronauts travel	__ **p a** __ __

2. Urp! Ugh! Ick! Swamp scum ruined some of the letters in the words below.

a coin	__ **i c k** __ __
something that jokes make you do	__ __ **u g h**
a color	__ **u r p** __ __
a bird that lays eggs that people eat	__ __ **i c k** __ __

3. Army ants marched through these words and ate some of the letters.

male deer have them	**a n t** __ __ __
Jack saw him at the top of the beanstalk	__ __ **a n t**
to put seeds in the ground	__ __ **a n t**
a very large animal	__ __ __ __ __ **a n t**

Name _____

Date _____

Great States

Every state in the United States has a postal abbreviation. It is made up of two letters from the state's name. Here are the postal abbreviations for six states.

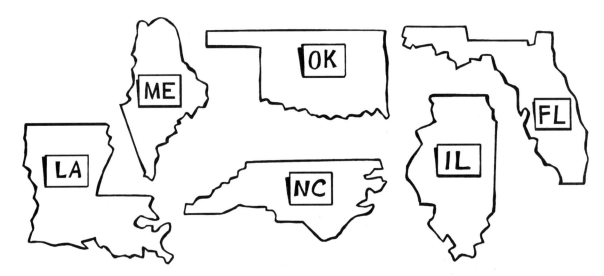

Using lowercase letters, write the letters of one of the six postal abbreviations on each of the lines to complete these common words.

1. br _ok_ e

2. h ____ l

3. f ____ m

4. fe ____ e

5. i ____ h

6. ____ al

7. ____ ag

8. ca ____ l

9. ____ ugh

10. ____ rge

11. sho ____

12. waf ____ e

Bonus! The postal abbreviation for Indiana is IN. On the lines below, write six words that have this letter combination in them at the front, the middle, or the end.

_____ _____ _____

_____ _____ _____

Activities for Fast Finishers: Language Arts © 2010 by Jan Meyer, Scholastic Teaching Resources

Name _____

Date _____

Monkey in the Middle

Each of these monkeys is holding a pair of letters you can use to make new words. Use the letters to the left of the monkey to begin the words and the letters to the right of the monkey to end them. You can use the beginning and ending letters more than once.

1.
b   **an**   e
h   g
s   k
l   d

hand
lane
_____
_____
_____

2.
f   **oo**   k
w   t
c   d
h   l

_____
_____
_____
_____
_____

3.
b   **ea**   l
h   r
d   t
r   d

_____
_____
_____
_____

4.
f   **ai**   d
m   l
s   n
p   r

_____
_____
_____
_____

Name _____

Date _____

A Secret Code

Spies use secret codes and now you can, too. Crack this code and you'll find the names for eight parts of the body.

TIPS

* Numbers have been substituted for the correct letters.

* The substituted numbers remain the same. For example: if **8** represents **f** in one word, **8** will represent **f** in all of the words in the group.

* Record the decoded letters on the correct blanks of all the rows. That will make decoding the remaining words easier.

PARTS OF THE BODY

1. h   e   a   d
   19 22 26 23

2. h   __ __ d
   19 26 13 23

3. __ __ __
   22 2   22

4. __ __ __ __
   16 13 22 22

5. __ __ __
   22 26 9

6. __ __ __ __ __
   19 22 26 9   7

7. __ __ __ __ __
   7   22 22 7   19

8. __ __ __ __ __ __
   7   19 9   12 26 7

Bonus! Here's a different code. Share it with your friends and write secret messages to each other.

a	b	c	d	e	f	g	h	i	j	k	l	m
2	1	4	3	6	5	8	7	10	9	12	11	14

n	o	p	q	r	s	t	u	v	w	x	y	z
13	16	15	18	17	20	19	22	21	24	23	26	25

Activities for Fast Finishers: Language Arts © 2010 by Jan Meyer, Scholastic Teaching Resources

Name _____

Date _____

Zig-Zag Word Chains

These word chains zig one way and then zag another way. They link together, though, because each new word that you add to the chain must begin with the last letter of the word before it. Add four-letter words to complete these chains. Words follow the squares across or down.

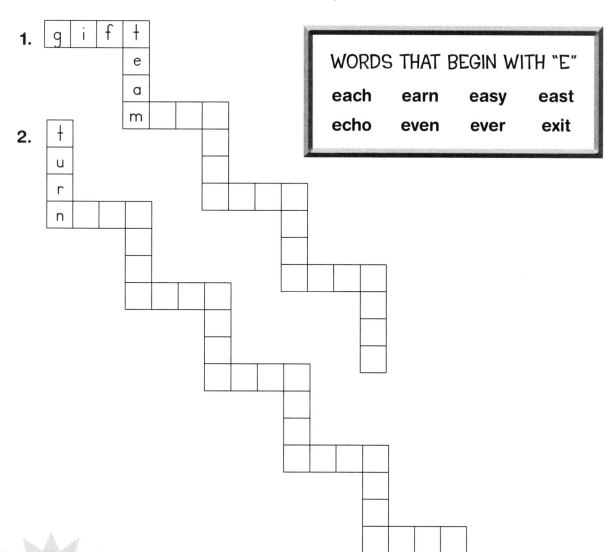

1. gift / team / m...

2. turn / ...

WORDS THAT BEGIN WITH "E"

each	earn	easy	east
echo	even	ever	exit

Bonus! For each chain, pick at least two words and use them in a sentence.

_____

_____

Name _____

Date _____

Wordy Wigglers

These wiggly caterpillars are filled with overlapping words and with words within words. Using the letters inside each caterpillar, make as many words of three or more letters as you can. All of the words are made with letters that are in order and next to each other.

1.

jobroomouthistarmanyear

Can you find at least 8 more?

job   broom   _____   _____   _____

_____   _____   _____   _____   _____

2.

baddresshiplanetrimask

Can you find at least 10?

_____   _____   _____   _____   _____

_____   _____   _____   _____   _____

Bonus!

fathereacheatapearthink

Can you find at least 15?

_____   _____   _____   _____   _____

_____   _____   _____   _____   _____

_____   _____   _____   _____   _____

Nice Mice and Lucky Duckies

Write the rhyming word pairs to answer each of the hink-pinks and hinky-pinkies. You'll find the words for the answers in the box to the right.

queen	tale	mad	spent
snake	candy	cent	fake
pretty	clean	dad	bunny
kitty	sandy	funny	whale

1. What do you call a wiggly reptile made of rubber?

_____

2. What do call an angry father?

_____

3. What do you call a young cat that is good-looking?

_____

4. What do you call a chocolate bar that's been dropped at the beach?

_____

5. What do you call a story about a very large mammal that lives in the ocean?

_____

6. What do you call the wife of a king who's just taken a bath?

_____

7. What do you call a penny that's been used to buy something?

_____

8. What do you call a young rabbit that tells jokes?

_____

HINK-PINK

A pair of one-syllable rhyming words that relate to a definition

EXAMPLE: nice mice

HINKY-PINKY

A pair of two-syllable rhyming words that relate to a definition

EXAMPLE: lucky duckies

Name _____

Date _____

Oh, No!

The Wizard of Oh wants to change all the vowels in these words to the vowel **o**. But if he does, will all of the words still make sense? Oh, no! I don't think so. In each row, circle the only word that won't work with the new spelling.

EXAMPLE: blew   less   (plant)   teeth

Blew would become *blow*, *less* would become *loss*,
teeth would become *tooth*. All are words.
Plant is circled because *plont* is not a word.

1.	hit	swing	drip	bald
2.	rub	dig	small	beat
3.	must	flash	fail	sing
4.	ring	seen	barn	pet
5.	ship	luck	leap	think
6.	dull	send	shirt	tea
7.	sift	click	blind	stir
8.	feed	mean	snack	last
9.	bath	best	park	knew
10.	slam	pair	farm	spit

Activities for Fast Finishers: Language Arts © 2010 by Jan Meyer, Scholastic Teaching Resources

Name _____

Date _____

Add a Letter and Stir

Here's a recipe for writing the names of different animals. To get started, add the mixed-up letters together and stir them up in your imagination. When you've thought of an animal whose name is made up of those letters, record the answer on the line.

Example: r e d + e = ___deer___

1. l a m e + c = _____

2. b a r e + z = _____

3. h o r n + i = _____

4. t i r e + g = _____

5. s o m e + u = _____

6. r o s e + h = _____

7. h e a l + w = _____

8. b r a v e + e = _____

Bonus! Put the letters of the two words together and then stir around all of the letters to create the name of an animal.

a. b a r + b i t ___ ___ b ___ i ___

b. f e a r + f i g ___ ___ ___ ___ f ___ ___

c. t h e + p l a n e ___ l ___ p ___ ___ ___ ___

Take a Look Inside

Inside each of these words is a shorter word with three or more letters. Circle the shorter word. Make sure the word is spelled correctly, with its letters in the correct order.

1. s(ever)al

2. g a r b a g e

3. m o n e y

4. p i e c e

5. m e a s u r e

6. b r e a d

7. a l p h a b e t

8. d e s i g n

9. o c t o p u s

10. f r i e n d

11. s t r e e t

12. m a c h i n e

13. m a c a r o n i

14. m o s q u i t o

15. j u i c e

16. o r c h e s t r a

Bonus! Write a sentence using two or more of the words that you circled.

_____

_____

Activities for Fast Finishers: Language Arts © 2010 by Jan Meyer, Scholastic Teaching Resources

Some, Many, or All

Using the letters of each word below, make as many words of three or more letters as you can. For each word you make, use the letters from the original word in any order, but use them only once.

1. thorn   Can you find at least six common words?

_____   _____

_____   _____

_____   _____

2. great   Can you find at least six common words?

_____   _____

_____   _____

_____   _____

Bonus!

Washington   Using the last name of our first President, try finding at least ten words.

_____   _____

_____   _____

_____   _____

_____   _____

_____   _____

A big cheer for you if you can find any five-letter words!

Name _____

Date _____

Don't Forget...

Mimi has written a shopping list, but she's written it in a special code. Use the grid below to find each of the letters until you've recorded all the items on her list. Write the correct letters on the blanks above the code letters as you find them.

	1	2	3	4	5
A	m	g	l	e	n
B	v	a	s	w	u
C	d	r	k	h	o
D	i	q	t	y	f
E	b	p	z	c	j

• EXAMPLE •

B4 is the letter **w**

D5 is the letter **f**

A2 is the letter **g**

SHOPPING LIST

1. m   i __ __
    A1 D1 A3 C3

2. __ __ __ __ __ __ __
    E2 A4 B2 E4 C4 A4 B3

3. __ __ __ __ __
    E5 A4 A3 A3 D4

4. __ __ __ __ __ __
    E4 A4 C2 A4 B2 A3

5. __ __ __ __ __
    E1 C2 A4 B2 C1

6. __ __ __ __ __ __ __
    E4 C4 D1 E4 C3 A4 A5

7. __ __ __ __ __ __ __
    B3 E2 D1 A5 B2 E4 C4

8. __ __ __ __ __ __ __
    C5 C2 B2 A5 A2 A4 B3

Activities for Fast Finishers: Language Arts © 2010 by Jan Meyer, Scholastic Teaching Resources

Letter Switcheroo

Look at the words in bold and the descriptions that follow them. To fill in the blanks, switch just any one letter from the previous answer and record the new answer on the spaces. Keep doing the switcheroo until all the answers are filled in.

1. an unhappy look   f r o w n

    a color   b r o w n

    something a king wears   __ __ __ __ __

    a large group   __ __ __ __ __

    two noisy black birds   __ __ __ __ __

2. a fish part   s c a l e

    a synonym for frighten   __ __ __ __ __

    to make a homerun   __ __ __ __ __

    a place to shop   __ __ __ __ __

    heavy rain with thunder and lightning   __ __ __ __ __

3. to yell   s h o u t

    what you do with a bow and an arrow   __ __ __ __ __

    an antonym for tall   __ __ __ __ __

    something to wear   __ __ __ __ __

    something else to wear   __ __ __ __ __

Name _____

Date _____

Whirl 'Em, Twirl 'Em, Swirl 'Em!

Read each given word and clue. Then whirl, twirl, and swirl the letters of each given word to make a word that goes with the clue. Record your answers in the chart.

GIVEN WORD	CLUE	ANSWER
1. grown	the opposite of *correct*	wrong
2. loop	a place to swim	
3. votes	it's found in a kitchen	
4. snoop	something to eat soup with	
5. wasp	a cat has four of them	
6. shore	an animal you can ride on	
7. shout	a compass direction	
8. steak	something to do on ice	
9. miles	a frown upside down	
10. elbow	the opposite of *above*	
11. nails	an animal that lives in its shell	
12. canoe	a large body of water	

Bonus! Make up your own word-and-clue set to whirl, twirl, and swirl!

_____ _____ _____

Activities for Fast Finishers: Language Arts © 2010 by Jan Meyer, Scholastic Teaching Resources

ANSWERS

Page 6
Norton's Nouns: lake, friend, hat, glasses, lion, circus, vegetable, glove;
Vera's Verbs: follow, eat, speak, bring, write, leave, ask, read

Page 7

	b	o	u	g	h	t			b	a	r	k	e	d
	u			e					r		o			
s	a	i	d						o		d	r	e	w
	i			r			c		k		e			a
	t			d	r	o	v	e						t
							o							c
		t	o	o	k									h
				e										e
	u	n	d	e	r	s	t	o	o	d				

Across
1. bought
3. barked
5. said
6. drew
9. drove
10. took
11. understood

Down
1. built
2. heard
3. broke
4. rode
7. watched
8. cooked

Page 8
First postcard should have circles around: Mr., Mrs., Moore, Maple, Drive, Newton, Maine, Dear, Aunt, Lisa, Uncle, Jeff, We're, Florida, Yesterday, Disneyland, The, March, Love, Jason;
Second postcard should have circles around: Tony, Milano, Baker, Street, Rockland, Ohio, Hi, Tony, New York, On, Friday, Museum of Natural History, The, Keesha, I, Yesterday, Thanksgiving, There, Santa Claus, Denzel

Page 9
Underlined: hear, cheer, dear, rear, here, clear, near, year, deer, fear
Circled: (across) rear, cheer, clear, deer, hear; (down) near, year, fear, dear, here

Page 10
1. eight, ate, wait
2. roll, hole, bowl
3. for, more, door, four
4. cry, eye, pie, high
5. two, blue, shoe, grew
6. hair, pear, care, where

Page 11
1. lamb
2. rock
3. honey
4. drum
5. balloon
6. sun
7. mountain
8. clown
9. elf
10. ice
Bonus! Answers will vary.

Page 12
Reasons will vary. Sample answers:
1. boots, scarf, mittens; They are all things to wear when it's cold.
2. kitten, lamb, piglet; They are all baby animals.
3. sofa, chair, stool; They are all things to sit on.
4. leaves, roots, stems; They are all parts of a plant.
5. barn, cow, scarecrow; They are all found on a farm.
6. Texas, Alaska, Florida; They are all states.

Page 13
1. sit
2. smell
3. hand
4. wood
5. scales
6. milk
7. princess
8. painting
9. goal
10. winter
Bonus! Answers will vary. Sample answers:
a. bark is to dog
b. corn is to vegetable

Page 14
Square (1-syllable words): stuff, ghost, earth, prize, dime
Circle (2-syllable words): table, winter, airplane, balloon, chicken
Rectangle (3-syllable words): alphabet, magician, crocodile, chimpanzee, calendar
Bonus! Answers will vary.

Page 15
Box 1: correct, carrot, napkin, mirror, picnic
Box 2: paper, blanket, monster, pillow, brother
Box 3: jungle, uncle, table, cradle, cattle

Page 16
1. was
2. I'm
3. not
4. here's
5. are
6. does
7. they've
8. we'll
9. have
10. let's
11. who's
12. you'd
13. have
14. we're

Page 17
The following places should have commas:
Sacramento, California
35,000,000
September 9, 1850
beaches, mountains, forests, and a large desert area
strawberries, lemons, walnuts, apricots, and grapes
Reno, Nevada
steep hills, cable cars, beautiful parks, and a place called Fisherman's Wharf
May 27, 1937

Page 18

1.
chat	cow	film
skunk	swing	tail
for	dust	dress

2.
place	goose	boy
crush	point	chief
smile	mean	hay

3.
steam	quick	meat
bark	glow	cute
quite	state	mouse

4.
stay	lunch	strength
wish	track	what
soup	bread	apple

5.
egg	print	hurt
quit	third	lost
dance	change	laugh

6.
right	cheese	ghost
through	school	worse
eight	sense	child

Page 19
1. skip, skill, skate
2. trade, trust, tree
3. swing, sweep, swim
4. clock, clown, clap
5. brush, brain, brick
6. steam, stop, store
7. slow, slide, slip
8. spot, speed, spell

Page 20
Answers will vary.

Page 21
1. The girls won their baseball game.
2. She wore her new sweater.
3. The cowboy rode on his horse.
4. The dog barked at the man.
5. That apple pie smells wonderful.
6. It was hot at the beach.
7. We're going to the amusement park.
8. An ant crawled up her arm.

Page 22
1. above
2. beach
3. brush
4. chart
5. dance
6. drink
7. dusty
8. every
9. first
10. fruit
Riddle answer: the outside

Page 23
1. magic
2. match
3. money
4. mouth
5. names
6. owner
7. panda
8. paste
9. patch
10. place
Riddle answer: a sandwitch

Page 24
Box 1: chipmunk, cockroach, cricket, coyote, cobra, clam, crab
Box 2: shark, skunk, snail, sponge, snake, shrimp, squid, spider, sheep

Page 25
please, every, again, family, should, answer, often, because, easy

Page 26
The following words should be circled and written correctly on the lines: friend, Tuesday, whose, minute, always, neighbor, dollar, birthday, among, address, receive, summer

Page 27
1. saving
2. looked
3. rub
4. live, lived
5. wish, wishing
6. learning, learned
7. stirring, stirred
8. dance, dancing
9. flip, flipped
10. baking, baked

Page 28
1. ss; lesson
2. gg; giggle
3. ff; traffic
4. rr; cherry
5. bb; bubble

6. dd; paddle
7. ff; muffin
8. bb; ribbon
9. tt; little
10. ll; yellow
Bonus! Answers will vary.

Page 29

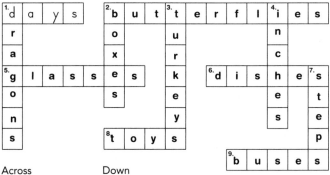

Across
1. days
2. butterflies
5. glasses
6. dishes
8. toys
9. buses

Down
1. dragons
2. boxes
3. turkeys
4. inches
7. steps

Page 30
1. easy
2. shout
3. start
4. large
5. pick
6. mad
7. fast
8. present
9. hard
10. scare
11. sick

Page 31
Ted's Terrific Tuesday
   Ted was feeling <u>happy</u>. Today was Amy's party and he was going to wear <u>new</u> jeans and a <u>clean</u> t-shirt. On his way to the party Ted <u>found</u> a five-dollar bill. When he arrived, <u>everyone</u> was <u>outside</u> playing games. The games were <u>exciting</u>. Ted was the <u>fastest</u> runner in the relay races and his team <u>won</u>.
   <u>After</u> the games, it was time to eat. Ted was <u>hungry</u>. He had pizza, a <u>big</u> piece of cake, and some <u>cold</u> lemonade. At the <u>end</u> of the party Ted said to Amy, "That was one of the <u>best</u> parties I've ever gone to. I'm <u>glad</u> I came."

Page 32
1. always, never, A
2. question, answer, A
3. part, piece, S
4. middle, center, S
5. tall, short, A
6. smart, intelligent, S
7. night, day, A
8. sink, float, A
9. stop, quit, S
10. asleep, awake, A
11. polite, rude, A
12. laugh, giggle, S
Bonus! Pictures will vary.

Page 33
1. tale, tail
2. bored, board
3. rode, road
4. threw, through
5. meet, meat
6. write, right
7. whether, weather
8. guessed, guest
Bonus! bare bear

Page 34
1. match
2. foot
3. ring
4. star
5. second
6. bark
7. pitcher
8. yard

Page 35

Page 36
1. teacup, teapot, teaspoon
2. snowman, snowflake, snowball
3. raincoat, rainbow, raindrop
4. toothache, toothpaste, toothbrush
5. bathtub, bathrobe, bathroom
6. football, footprint, footstep
7. doorbell, doorway, doorknob
8. suntan, sunshine, sunburn
9. airline, airplane, airport
10. fireworks, fireplace, firetruck
Bonus! Answers will vary.

Page 37
1. boring
2. amazed
3. very angry
4. smell
5. difficult
6. joyful

Page 38
Answers will vary.

Page 39
1. unhelpful
2. impatient
3. untied
4. incorrect
5. dishonest
6. impossible
7. disagree
8. unfair
Answer: on its front legs

Page 40
1. fearful
2. powerless
3. poisonous
4. painful
5. careless
6. dangerous
7. colorful
8. thankful
Answer: an elephant

Page 41
1. battery
2. steel
3. mother
4. million
5. bowling
6. beard
7. coward
8. rattle
9. grape
10. crowd
11. kitchen
12. vacation

Page 42
Fruit section: grapes, banana, apple, pear, melon; orange
Pet section: kitten, fish, bunny, hamster, parrot; snake

Page 43
Answers will vary. Sample answers:
1. fight, gift, fit, it
2. wrong, grow, row, or
3. stone, nose, son, on
4. white, with, hit, it
5. floor, roof, for, of
6. watch what, hat, at

Page 44
1. bowl
2. east
3. ring
4. seal
5. chin
6. ape
7. rose
8. lamp
9. wolf
10. flea

Page 45

h	v	p	u	w
b	z	l	j	a
r	f	o	c	n
i	k	m	o	d
e	t	g	q	s

Answer: blood

Page 46

Answers may vary. Sample answers:
1. b + east = beast
2. plan + t = plant
3. thin + k = think
4. s + care = scare
5. hear + d = heard
6. b + room = broom
7. crow + n = crown
8. star + e = stare
9. b + read = bread
10. t + each = teach
Bonus!
a. w + hole = whole
b. toot + h = tooth

Page 47
1. stomach, palace, pajamas, paper space
2. nickel, laugh, purple, chicken
3. antlers, giant, plant, elephant

Page 48
1. broke
2. hill
3. film
4. fence
5. inch
6. meal
7. flag
8. camel
9. laugh
10. large
11. shook
12. waffle
Bonus! Answers will vary.

Page 49
Answers will vary. Sample answers:
1. bang, bank, band, hang, hand, sang, sank, sand, lane, land
2. foot, food, fool, wood, wool, cook, cool, hook, hoot, hood
3. bear, beat, bead, hear, heat, heal, head, deal, dear, real, read
4. fail, fair, maid, mail, main, said, sail, paid, pail, pain, pair

Page 50
1. head
2. hand
3. eye
4. knee
5. ear
6. heart
7. teeth
8. throat
Bonus! Answers will vary.

Page 51
Answers will vary.

Page 52
1. job, broom, room, mouth, out, this, his, star, tar, arm, man, many, any, year, ear
2. bad, add, address, dress, ship, hip, plan, plane, lane, planet, net, trim, rim, mask, ask

Bonus! fat, father, the, there, her, here, reach, each ache, cheat, heat, eat, tap, tape, ape, pea, pear, ear, art, earth, thin, think, ink

Page 53
1. fake snake
2. mad dad
3. pretty kitty
4. sandy candy
5. whale tale
6. clean queen
7. spent cent
8. funny bunny

Page 54
1. swing
2. small
3. flash
4. ring
5. think
6. send
7. stir
8. snack
9. best
10. slam

Page 55
1. camel
2. zebra
3. rhino
4. tiger
5. mouse
6. horse
7. whale
8. beaver
Bonus!
a. rabbit
b. giraffe
c. elephant

Page 56
1. ever
2. bag
3. one
4. pie
5. sure
6. read
7. bet
8. sign
9. top
10. end
11. tree
12. chin
13. car
14. quit
15. ice
16. chest
Bonus! Answers will vary.

Page 57
Answers will vary. Sample answers:
1. ton, torn, horn, hot, rot, nor, not, north
2. gate, gear, get, rag, rage, rat, rate, ear, eat, age, are, art, ate, tag, tar, tea, tear
Bonus! wag, waist, want, was, wash, what, wig, win, wing wish, with, won,

sag, sang, sat, saw, shin, sigh, sin, sing, sit, snag, snow, son, song, sow, stain, sting, stow, swan, swang, swat, swing, hang, has, hat, hint, his, hot, how, inn, its, not, nothing, now, gain, gas, ghost, got, tag, tan, tang, than, thaw, thin, thing, this, tin, ton, tow, town, twig, twin, oat, own

Page 58
1. milk
2. peaches
3. jelly
4. cereal
5. bread
6. chicken
7. spinach
8. oranges

Page 59
1. frown, brown, crown, crowd, crows
2. scale, scare, score, store, storm
3. shout, shoot, short, shirt, skirt

Page 60
1. wrong
2. pool
3. stove
4. spoon
5. paws
6. horse
7. south
8. skate
9. smile
10. below
11. snail
12. ocean
Bonus! Answers will vary.